GOAN FLAVOURS

Rita Gonsalves

AuthorHouse™ UK Ltd.
500 Avebury Boulevard
Central Milton Keynes, MK9 2BE
www.authorhouse.co.uk
Phone: 08001974150

©2009 Rita Gonsalves. All rights reserved.

No part of this book may be reproduced, stored in a retrieval system, or transmitted by any means without the written permission of the author.

First published by AuthorHouse 7/21/2009

ISBN: 978-1-4490-0889-5 (sc)

This book is printed on acid-free paper.

This little book of recipes is affectionately dedicated to my dearest Mum, Sophie Gonsalves

Contents

Snacks 1
Soups 12
Fish 18
Chicken 27
Meat 35
Vegetarian 49
Rice 68
Desserts 76
Goan Sweets 85

Introduction

GLORIOUS GOA – think abundant rich vegetation, iridescent butterflies and birds, glittering fish in shimmering seas. This unique place was discovered by Portuguese travellers in their quest for a New Continent, and though they are long departed, their customs, architecture, and cuisine provide a prominent legacy.

It was my grandmother, known to everyone in the village as "Mae", who first instilled in me the idea that cooking could be enjoyable – something worth taking pride in. As a youngster I would watch her singing as she stirred huge pots over the wood fire in our outdoor kitchen. The idea of cooking without electricity may scare us now, but the smoky flavour of the food was distinctive and delicious. The kitchen was always a fabulous hive of activity – my mother and grandmother debating over how best to chop the fresh vegetables, or grinding spicy masalas on a large granite slab whilst the other grated coconuts, and my father and brothers dropping in to help draw water from our well to nurture our precious coconut saplings. Then, if one of us had been misbehaving, we'd be guaranteed the job of spending the afternoon guarding our rice crop from crows as it dried on straw mats beside our house.

Often I would spend my time helping my mother, Sophie, and Mae in our large garden. Although we spoke English at home, they would endeavour to teach me the local Goan language, *Konkani,* which is still widely used in the state today. I fondly remember helping shell the large green peas as my mother and grandmother picked them – that is if I hadn't disappeared to climb a tree to beat my brothers to the best fruit.

The best season for fruit in Goa falls in April and May. Those months hold so many great memories for me and the many others who would arrive from neighbouring states to enjoy this bountiful time, naturally also making the most of the hot weather with trips to the many golden beaches. In the evenings my friends and I would venture into the hills behind our village, returning at the sound of the Angelus bells with baskets laden with fruit.

Goa is also well known for the humble cashew seed, which is arguably its most famous export. The cashew-bearing tree's irregular-shaped trunk and the large dark evergreen leaves make it easily recognisable in the Goan landscape. Whilst the fruit of the tree is tasty eaten with a pinch of salt, it is more commonly found in its distilled form – a potent, locally brewed liquor called cashew feni. The seeds (generally referred to as "nuts") have a myriad of uses, delicious eaten roasted or spiced, in a curry or along with a good bottle of Kingfisher beer.

My mother is now a highly acclaimed cook in her own right, who together with my father, Domingos, always loved to entertain guests for dinner. Helping them lay out huge, traditional spreads has certainly influenced my enthusiasm for cooking. I love organising dinner parties at my home – bringing a taste of Goa to Surrey! – and now wish to share my recipes with you. Many of the ingredients are said to have medicinal value, so they are a treat for your body as well as your taste buds. I have done my best to modify them to suit Western kitchens and save a little time, whilst ensuring that the authentic Goan flavours are still captured.

Monsoons in Goa

For me, the monsoons in Goa are synonymous with the delicious, fluffy rice we enjoyed with every meal. When the monsoon reigns between June and September, the Goan landscape is transformed and truly reaches the height of its beauty. During those months the rice crop is grown, causing field upon field to turn into a shimmering green carpet.

The harvesting of the rice is a tedious process and involves days spent gathering, storing and drying the grain before it is taken to the local mill to have the husks removed. The versatility and fantastic taste of the rice always makes it worthwhile though!

Goa has a wonderful range of beautiful flowering trees and plants, filling the place with colour. Here are some that grow in our garden.

A few more fruit trees in our garden

Breadfruit Tree

Bimblis – sour fruit mainly used to flavour curries

The Humble Coconut Tree

In Britain they could not live without the humble potato, however, in Goa it is the humble coconut tree that is essential to life. No part of the tree can be said to be wasted.

In most Goan dishes you will find that the flesh or the milk of the coconut is used. But its usefulness does not stop there. The huge leaves of the palm tree are used in a number of ways. Most famously, one could see grandmothers and aunties on porches everywhere just before the monsoons 'knitting' the tough leaves into shelters to protect homes from the coming heavy rain and strong winds.

A creamy, sweet oil can also be extracted from the fruit, which is great for both cooking and massages.

Also, the inner veins of the leaves, when stripped of foliage, can be used to make strong brooms. The husks of the coconut are still used today for cleaning (a natural answer to the scrubbing brush!) or as fuel for the cooking fire.

Showing that they even have a commercial value, the coconut shells can now often be seen as fabulous ornaments to impress and amuse tourists, alongside bottles of the potent, local liquor – coconut feni.

Sweet Rice Noodles

This is another sweet dish that used to be served during the monsoons at tea time. Below is a picture of the appliance that was used to make the noodles, and I have fond memories of my grandmother using it. The rice noodles would then be mixed with fresh coconut and jaggery, the taste was just delicious!

Old fashioned noodle maker

Coconut grater

Stone grinder which now adorns our garden |

Old fashioned steamer (komfro)

Snacks

Crab Quiche

Spicy Mince Burgers

Onion/Chilli Bhajas

Coriander Chutney

Samosas

Patties

Savoury Vegetables

Potato Chops

Corn on the Cob

Omelette Bites

Crab Quiche

Ingredients

For the Pastry
225 g plain flour
pinch of salt
100 g margarine or butter
3–4 tbsp cold water

For the Filling
1 tbsp olive oil
2 medium onions, chopped
1 tsp curry powder
1 tbsp coriander leaves, chopped
2 tins (340g) crabmeat, drained
3 eggs
¾ pt milk
salt & pepper to taste
2 tbsp cheese, grated

Make the pastry by mixing flour and salt in a large bowl. Rub in the butter or margarine until you have a soft crumbly texture. Add a bit of cold water and knead until the mixture forms a firm dough. Lightly grease a flan dish with a very small amount of butter, roll out the pastry on a lightly floured surface and place into the flan dish. Trim the edges and bake blind for 10 minutes.

To prepare the filling, heat the oil and sauté the onions, curry powder, and coriander leaves for a couple of minutes. Then spread this mixture evenly over the pastry, followed by the crabmeat. In a separate bowl, whisk the eggs. Add milk, salt and pepper and pour evenly into the dish. Sprinkle with grated cheese and bake in the oven at 180°C/350°F/gas mark 4 for 30 minutes.

Preparation time: 30 minutes
Cooking time: 40 minutes

Spicy Mince Burgers

Ingredients

1 kg mince
2 onions, finely chopped
2 green chillies, finely chopped
1 tsp crushed ginger
6 cloves crushed garlic
1 tsp cumin powder
1 tbsp coriander powder
1 egg
1 tbsp lemon juice
2 tbsp coriander leaves, finely chopped
2 slices of bread (soaked in water & drained)
2 tbsp cider vinegar
pinch of pepper powder
pinch of red chilli powder
salt to taste

1 cup semolina (for the coating)
2 tbsp olive oil for frying

Mix all the ingredients together and form into burgers. Coat each side with semolina and fry in a non-stick pan on both sides until lightly brown. Makes around 20 burgers.

Preparation time: 20 minutes
Cooking time: 20 minutes

Onion/Chilli Bhajas

Ingredients

2 onions, finely chopped
250 g gram flour
pinch of baking powder
pinch of red chilli powder
½ tsp cumin powder
1 large green chilly, finely chopped
2 tbsp coriander leaves, finely chopped
juice of ½ lemon
10 fl oz water
salt to taste
oil for frying

Mix all the ingredients to form a thick paste. Deep fry in hot oil until golden brown. For a spicy twist, try dipping chillies in the paste and deep fry until golden brown. Serve with coriander chutney.

Preparation time: 10 minutes
Cooking time: 15 minutes

Coriander Chutney

(Excellent with chappatis, bhajas, or in sandwiches)

Ingredients

2 cups coriander leaves
50 g coconut cream
2 green chillies
pinch of cinnamon powder
½ tsp cumin powder
1 tsp sugar
4 cloves garlic
¼-inch piece of ginger
1 onion, chopped
2 tbsp lemon juice
2 tbsp water

Put all the ingredients in a blender or grinder for 5 minutes or until mixture has turned into a fine paste.

Preparation time: 15 minutes

Samosas

Ingredients

½ kg minced beef OR soya mince
1 onion, finely chopped
1 tsp crushed ginger
4 cloves crushed garlic
1 green chilli, finely chopped
½ tsp turmeric powder
½ tsp cumin powder
1 tbsp coriander powder
1 tbsp tomato puree
pinch of chilli powder
2 tbsp coriander leaves, finely chopped
½ cup water
salt & pepper to taste

For the Pastry

400 g plain flour
2 tbsp olive oil
½ cup water
pinch of salt

Oil for frying

Fry the mince over a low heat and drain off all the fat. Stir in the chopped onion and the rest of the ingredients. Add water and simmer for 15 minutes, stirring occasionally until the mixture is almost dry. Set aside to cool.

Prepare the pastry mixture by mixing the flour, oil, salt, and water, and kneading it into a soft dough. Divide into small balls. Roll a ball on a floured surface to make a circle of approximately 7 inches in diameter. Cut the circle in half. Then take one half and fold it to make a cone. Using your fingertip, seal the edges with a dab of water. Fill the cone with the stuffing and close, sealing the edges with a little water. Deep fry until golden brown.

Preparation time: 50 minutes
Cooking time: 20 minutes

Patties

Using the same ingredients as on the opposite page, patties can be made by using ready-made puff pastry, rolling the dough on a board, cutting it into rectangles, and filling in with 1 tablespoon of mince. Paste sides with a dab of water and bake in the oven at 180°C/350°F/gas mark 4.

Preparation time: 30 minutes
Cooking time: 30 minutes

Savoury Vegetables

Ingredients

1 tsp curry powder
salt to taste
½ cup peas
1 carrot, diced
2 small potatoes, diced
1 small tin (140g) sweetcorn, drained
1 tbsp mayonnaise
fresh coriander leaves, chopped (for garnish)

In a pan of boiling water, add the curry powder, salt, and peas and cook for 5 minutes. Then add the carrot and potatoes and cook for a further 5 minutes. (Do not allow to overcook). Drain and set aside to cool. Add the sweetcorn and mayonnaise to the cooled vegetables. This mixture can be spooned onto crackers or toasties just before serving. Garnish with fresh chopped coriander leaves.

Preparation time: 10 minutes
Cooking time: 10 minutes

Potato Chops

Ingredients

½ kg soya mince OR beef mince
1 onion, finely chopped
1 tsp crushed ginger
4 cloves crushed garlic
2 green chillies, finely chopped
½ tsp turmeric powder
½ tsp cumin powder
1 tbsp coriander powder
1 tbsp tomato puree
pinch of chilli powder
2 tbsp coriander leaves, chopped
½ cup water
salt & pepper to taste

1 kg potatoes, boiled and mashed

For the Coating
2 eggs, beaten
1 cup semolina
Oil for frying

Fry the mince on a low heat and drain off all the fat. Add chopped onion and the rest of the ingredients and stir for a few minutes. Add water and simmer for 15 minutes, stirring occasionally, until the mixture is almost dry. Set aside to cool.

When both the potato and mince are slightly cool, place a small bit of potato into the palm of your hand and make a cup. Add one teaspoon of mince into it and cover using some more potato and form a round chop. Dip into the beaten egg, coat with semolina, and lightly fry on both sides until golden brown.

Preparation time: 45 minutes
Cooking time: 20 minutes

Corn on the Cob

Ingredients

4 cobs of corn
½ fresh lemon or lime
pinch of chilli powder
salt to taste

Remove outer leaves and place the corn in a pan of water. Add a little bit of salt and boil the corn for 10 minutes, or until cooked. Drain and leave to cool. Before serving, rub the lemon juice across the corn and sprinkle with a bit of mild chilli powder.

Preparation time: 5 minutes
Cooking time: 10 minutes

Omelette Bites

Ingredients

2 eggs
salt and pepper to taste
1 onion, finely chopped
1 green chilli, finely chopped
1 tbsp coriander leaves, finely chopped
1 tbsp olive oil
cheese slices for topping

Whisk the eggs with a bit of salt and pepper until light and fluffy, then add the onion, green chilli, and coriander leaves. Heat the oil in a non-stick pan and fry the omelette on both sides until golden brown. Slice into rectangles and set aside to cool. Serve on crackers or sliced bread with a piece of cheese for the topping.

Preparation time: 10 minutes
Cooking time: 5 minutes

Soups

Pez (Rice Soup)

Macaroni Soup

Vegetable Soup

Tomato & Orange Soup

Pumpkin Soup

Rice Soup – Pez – Kanji

This popular soup called '*Pez*' was served in most Goan homes around eleven in the morning. This is a simple and nourishing rice soup, cooked in a clay pot with the paddy rice grown in the local fields. This is most delicious when eaten with raw mango water pickle, fresh grated coconut, or curry left over from the night before (*kalchi koddi*).

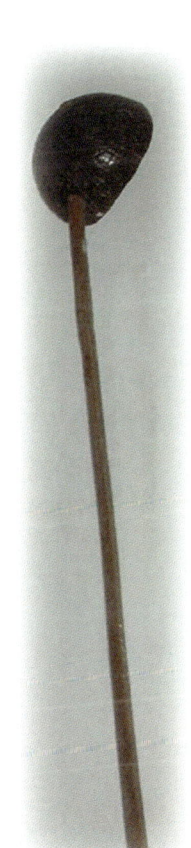

Ingredients

4 cups water
1 cup Goan rice
salt to taste

Bring the water to the boil, add the washed rice and salt, and cook for 30 minutes until rice is soft. Do not drain the water.

Macaroni Soup

Ingredients

1 onion, finely chopped
1 tbsp olive oil
2 pints water
1 stock cube (chicken or vegetable)
pinch of chilli powder
pinch of turmeric powder
½ tsp dried basil
1 tbsp dried fenugreek leaves
½ cup macaroni or other pasta
2 carrots, diced

Fry the onion in olive oil until lightly browned, then add water, stock cube, and all the spices. When the stock cube has dissolved, add the carrots and pasta. Bring to the boil and simmer until pasta is cooked.

Preparation time: 10 minutes
Cooking time: 20 minutes

Vegetable Soup

Ingredients

1 onion, chopped
2 tablespoons olive oil
2 pints water
1 stock cube (chicken or vegetable)
1 tbsp dried fenugreek leaves
2 cloves crushed garlic
¼ tsp turmeric powder
½ tsp dried basil
pinch of chilli powder
salt & pepper to taste
2 carrots, sliced
4 potatoes, diced
2 leeks, chopped

Fry the onion in olive oil until lightly browned, then add water, stock cube, and spices. When the stock cube has dissolved, add the vegetables, bring to the boil, then simmer for 15 minutes.

Preparation time: 15 minutes
Cooking time: 20 minutes

Tomato & Orange Soup

Ingredients

1 onion, chopped
1 tbsp olive oil
2 pints water
1 stock cube (chicken or vegetable)
1 large orange
2 carrots, sliced
2 potatoes, diced
1 tin (400g) tomatoes, chopped
½ tsp turmeric powder
¼ tsp paprika powder
1 tsp coriander leaves, chopped
salt & pepper to taste

Fry the onion in olive oil until lightly browned, then add water and stock cube. Cut the orange into 4 segments, remove outside peel and place peel in the pan of water. When the stock cube has dissolved, add the vegetables and spices. Bring to the boil, then simmer for 10 minutes. Deseed the orange, cut finely, and add to the pan. Remove the orange peel segments before serving.

Preparation time: 10 minutes
Cooking time: 15 minutes

Pumpkin Soup

Ingredients

1 onion, chopped
1 tbsp olive oil
2 pints water
1 stock cube (chicken or vegetable)
½ tsp dried basil leaves
pinch of chilli powder
pinch of turmeric powder
1 tbsp desiccated coconut
salt & pepper to taste
1 small pumpkin, cubed
2 carrots, diced
2 potatoes, diced

Fry the onion in olive oil until lightly browned, then add the water, stock cube, and spices. When the stock cube has dissolved, add the vegetables. Bring to the boil, then simmer for 15 minutes. This soup can be liquidised. Serve with garlic bread.

Preparation time: 15 minutes
Cooking time: 20 minutes

Fish

Prawn Curry

Salmon Curry

Fried Sardines

Spiced and Grilled Mackerels or Pomfrets

Mackerel Cutlets

Sour Fish Curry

Prawn Chilli Fry

Fish

Goa being on the coastal belt, fish is in abundance. It is indeed a wondrous thing to watch the fishing boats come into the shore and drawing out the nets with their haul. So many varieties can be seen in their nets – crabs, oysters, mussels, prawns, pomfret, mackerel, kingfish, sardines, squid, lobsters, and much more. As the staple diet is rice and fish, there are a variety of ways that the fish is prepared.

Prawn Curry

This dish has proved a winner time and time again!

Ingredients

2 tbsp olive oil
1 onion, finely chopped
1 tbsp coriander powder
½ tsp cumin powder
½ tsp turmeric powder
1 tsp crushed ginger
2 cloves crushed garlic
salt & pepper to taste
½ cup water
50 g coconut cream
300 g frozen prawns (fresh can be used too)
1 green chilli sliced lengthways
2 tbsp tomato puree
2 tbsp coriander leaves, chopped

Heat the oil and fry the onion until lightly browned, then add the spices and stir for a few seconds. Add water and coconut cream and stir until the coconut has melted. Add the prawns and the rest of the ingredients and cook on a low heat for 10 minutes, stirring occasionally.

Preparation time: 10 minutes
Cooking time: 12 minutes

Salmon Curry

Ingredients

2 tbsp olive oil
1 onion, finely chopped
½ tsp cumin powder
½ tsp turmeric powder
1 tbsp coriander powder
salt & pepper to taste
1 cup water
50 g coconut cream
2 tbsp tomato puree
1 green chilli, sliced lengthways
2 tbsp coriander leaves, finely chopped
4 salmon fillets

Heat the oil and fry the onion until lightly browned, then stir in the spices. Add water, coconut cream, tomato puree, green chilli, and coriander leaves. Simmer for 5 minutes until the coconut cream has dissolved. Gently place the salmon pieces into the pan and cook on one side for 4 minutes. Turn the fillets over and cook for a further 4 minutes. Be careful not to overcook or the fish will break up.

Preparation time: 10 minutes
Cooking time: 15 minutes

Fried Sardines

Ingredients

2 tbsp semolina
1 tsp turmeric powder
pinch of chilli powder
10 sardines
1 egg, beaten
2 tbsp olive oil
salt & pepper to taste

Mix semolina with turmeric and chilli powder in a shallow dish. Dip sardines in the beaten egg and coat with the dry mix. Fry on a low heat until brown on both sides. Salt and pepper to taste.

Preparation time: 10 minutes
Cooking Time: 10 minutes

Spiced & Grilled Pomfrets or Mackerels

Ingredients

¼ tsp chilli powder
¼ tsp cumin powder
¼ tsp crushed ginger
2 cloves crushed garlic
¼ tsp black pepper powder
1 tbsp cider vinegar
1 tbsp lemon juice
4 mackerels or pomfrets
1 tbsp olive oil
salt to taste

Combine the spices and mix in the vinegar and lemon juice to form a thick paste. Make a slit along the top of the fish and stuff it with the paste. Dab the outside of the fish with a bit of olive oil and a sprinkling of salt and place under the grill for 5 minutes. Turn over and grill for another 5 minutes. This dish can also be baked in the oven for 30 minutes.

Preparation time: 10 minutes
Cooking time: 10 minutes

Mackerel Cutlets

Ingredients

4 mackerels
1 onion, finely chopped
1 green chilli, finely chopped
2 cloves crushed garlic
½ tsp crushed ginger
½ tsp cumin powder
1 tsp coriander powder
pinch of chilli powder
1 egg
2 tbsp cider vinegar
2 tbsp coriander leaves, finely chopped
salt & pepper to taste

For the Coating
2 tbsp semolina
2 tbsp oil for frying

Cover the mackerels in water and boil for 10 minutes, then set aside to cool. Debone the fish and mix with the rest of the ingredients. Shape into cutlets. Coat each piece with the semolina and fry to a light golden brown, turning over so both sides are done.

Preparation time: 30 minutes
Cooking time: 10 minutes

Sour Fish Curry

Ingredients

1 onion, finely chopped
2 tbsp olive oil
1 tsp chilli powder
½ tsp cumin powder
½ tsp turmeric powder
½ tsp crushed ginger
3 cloves crushed garlic
½ tsp clove powder
2 tbsp tamarind paste
2 tbsp cider vinegar
½ cup water
1 large fish, thickly sliced
salt to taste

Fry the onion in olive oil until lightly browned, then stir in the spices and the rest of the ingredients. Lastly add the fish and cook on a low heat, stirring occasionally. Salt to taste.

Preparation time: 10 minutes
Cooking time: 15 minutes

Prawn Chilly Fry

Ingredients

2 onions, finely chopped
2 tbsp olive oil
300 g frozen prawns (fresh can be used too)
½ tsp turmeric powder
½ tsp chilli powder
2 cloves crushed garlic
1 tsp crushed ginger
1 green chilli, sliced lengthways
1 tbsp coriander leaves, finely chopped
1 red bell pepper, diced
salt & pepper to taste

Fry the onions in olive oil until lightly browned, then add the prawns and the rest of the ingredients. Gently fry, stirring continuously until prawns are cooked.

Preparation time: 10 minutes
Cooking time: 12 minutes

Chicken

Coriander Chicken

Chicken Xacuti

Breaded Chicken/Turkey Fillets

Chicken in a Spicy Tomato Sauce

Chicken Curry

Spiced Chicken Drumsticks

Roast Chicken

Coriander Chicken

Ingredients

1 tsp crushed ginger
4 cloves crushed garlic
½ tsp clove powder
½ tsp cinnamon powder
½ tsp cardamom powder
½ tsp chilli powder
4 tbsp coriander leaves, chopped
2 tbsp lemon juice
1 tbsp cider vinegar
1 kg chicken pieces, skinned
1 onion, finely chopped
2 tbsp olive oil
1 ½ cups water
salt & pepper to taste

Mix all the spices with the vinegar and lemon juice. Apply mixture to the chicken pieces and marinate for at least one hour. Fry the onion in oil until lightly browned, then add the chicken and fry for a few seconds. Lastly add the water and cover. Leave to cook, stirring occasionally, until the chicken is tender and the liquid is nearly gone.

Preparation time: 15 minutes
Cooking time: 40 minutes

Chicken Xacuti

This dish gets its unique taste and flavour from the roasted coconut and spices and is prepared in stages.

Ingredients

1 tbsp coriander powder
1 tsp cumin powder
¼ tsp cinnamon powder
¼ tsp clove powder
¼ tsp ground black pepper
¼ tsp nutmeg powder
½ tsp chilli powder
1 cup fresh grated coconut
1 onion, finely chopped
2 tbsp olive oil

1 tsp crushed ginger
4 cloves crushed garlic
1 tsp caraway seeds
4 chicken breasts, cubed
½ tsp turmeric powder
1 green chilli, finely chopped
1 tbsp tamarind paste
4 stars anise
2 cups water
salt & pepper to taste

The first stage is to mix together the coriander, cumin, cinnamon, clove, pepper, nutmeg, and chilli powders and dry roast for a few seconds in a non-stick pan. Remove and set aside. In the same pan, dry roast the coconut and add to the spices. Next, fry the onion in oil until lightly browned. Add the ginger, garlic, and caraway seeds and fry for a few seconds, then mix in the chicken and the rest of the ingredients. Bring to the boil, then simmer until chicken is soft and tender. Salt and pepper to taste. Remove the star anise before serving.

Preparation time: 15 minutes
Cooking time: 30 minutes.

Breaded Chicken/Turkey Fillets

Ingredients

4 tbsp semolina
½ tsp turmeric powder
pinch of paprika powder
salt & pepper to taste
4 chicken or turkey fillets
1 egg (beaten)
2 tbsp olive oil

Mix together the semolina, turmeric, paprika, salt, and pepper. Dip the fillets in the beaten egg, then coat with the semolina mixture. Fry on both sides in oil until golden brown.

Preparation time: 10 minutes
Cooking time: 10 minutes

Chicken in a Spicy Tomato Sauce

Ingredients

1 tbsp olive oil
1 onion, finely chopped
1 ½ tbsp coriander powder
1 tsp cumin powder
½ tsp clove powder
½ tsp turmeric powder
½ tsp chilli powder
½ tsp nutmeg powder
½ tsp cinnamon powder
1 tsp crushed ginger
4 cloves crushed garlic
1 tbsp tamarind paste
salt to taste
1 tin (400g) tomatoes, chopped
50 g coconut cream
2 cups water
4 chicken thighs, skinned

Heat the oil and fry the onion until lightly browned, then stir in all the spices. Add the tinned tomatoes, coconut cream and water and bring to the boil. Lastly, add the chicken and cook until tender, stirring occasionally.

Preparation time: 15 minutes
Cooking time: 30 minutes

Chicken Curry

Ingredients

2 tbsp olive oil
2 onions, finely chopped
4 chicken breasts, diced
1 tsp cumin powder
2 tbsp coriander powder
½ tsp turmeric powder
1 tsp chilli powder
4 cloves crushed garlic
1 tsp crushed ginger
½ cup peas
1 tin (400g) tomatoes, chopped
50 g coconut cream
2 tbsp coriander leaves, chopped
1 cup water
salt to taste

Heat the oil, add the onions and chicken, and cook for 2 minutes, stirring continuously. Add the rest of the ingredients, bring to the boil, and then simmer for 15 minutes, stirring occasionally.

Preparation time: 10 minutes
Cooking time: 20 minutes

Spiced Chicken Drumsticks

Ingredients

1 tsp coriander powder
1 tsp cumin powder
¼ tsp turmeric powder
¼ tsp chilli powder
1 tsp crushed ginger
2 cloves crushed garlic
1 tbsp cider vinegar
3 tbsp olive oil
1 tbsp lemon juice
salt & pepper to taste
10 chicken drumsticks

Onion rings for garnish

Mix all the ingredients into a paste, apply to the chicken, and marinate for an hour. Cover with foil and roast in the oven, at 180°C/350°F/gas mark 4 for 45 minutes or until cooked. Decorate with onion rings.

Preparation time: 10 minutes
Cooking time: 45 minutes

Roast Chicken

Ingredients

4 cloves crushed garlic
1 tsp crushed ginger
½ tsp cumin powder
½ tsp turmeric powder
½ tsp clove powder
1 tbsp cider vinegar
2 tbsp lemon juice
2 tbsp olive oil
salt & pepper to taste
1 whole chicken, skinned

Mix all the ingredients together, apply to the chicken, and marinate for an hour (the longer the better). Place the chicken in the oven at 180°C/350°F/gas mark 4 and roast for 45 minutes on one side, turn over and roast for a further 45 minutes until it is cooked.

Preparation time: 10 minutes
Cooking time: 1hr 30 minutes

Meat

Pork Sorpotel & Sannas

Grilled Pork Chops

Pork Vindalho

Roast Pork

Roast Beef

Minced Beef Curry

Meat Ball Curry

Beef Chilli Fry

Lambs Liver

Lamb Curry

Lamb Biryani

Roast Lamb

Pork Sorpotel

Sorpotel is a festive dish, and in the past, it was prepared a few days in advance, in earthenware vessels over a wood fire. Vinegar was used as a preservative. In those days, when no electricity was available, this dish was heated once a day as a precaution. Sorpotel would always be accompanied by sannas (steamed rice muffins).

Ingredients

1 kg pork belly rashers
½ kg liver
2 green chillies, finely chopped
1 tsp crushed ginger
6 cloves crushed garlic
½ tsp chilli powder
1 tsp cumin powder
½ tsp black pepper powder
1 tbsp coriander powder
½ tsp turmeric powder
2 tsp tamarind paste
2 tbsp cider vinegar
salt to taste

Cover the pork and liver with water and boil for 10 minutes. Remove the meat from the water and set aside to cool. Put all the other ingredients in that same pan of water and simmer. Cut the pork and liver into small cubes and fry in its own fat for a couple of minutes, then add to the pan. Bring to the boil, then simmer for 30 minutes, stirring occasionally.

Preparation time: 20 minutes
Cooking time: 1 hour

Sannas (Steamed Rice Muffins)

Ingredients

2 cups rice flour
2 tsp dried yeast (or ½ bottle toddy)
1 cup desiccated coconut
1 tsp sugar
½ tsp salt
Dab of oil (for greasing ramekin dishes)

Mix all the ingredients together and leave in a warm place for half an hour till the batter has doubled in size. Grease the ramekin dishes and ladle in the batter. Steam for 30 minutes or until cooked.

Preparation time: 40 minutes (including standing time)
Cooking time: 30 minutes

Grilled Pork Chops

Ingredients

2 cloves crushed garlic
½ tsp crushed ginger
½ tsp turmeric powder
pinch of chilli powder
1 tbsp lemon juice
1 tbsp olive oil
salt & pepper to taste
3 pork chops

Mix all the ingredients into a paste and apply to the pork chops. Place under the grill and cook for 10 minutes on both sides

Preparation time: 10 minutes
Cooking time: 20 minutes

Pork Vindalho

Ingredients

2 large onions, finely chopped
2 tbsp olive oil
½ kg pork (cubed)
4 cloves crushed garlic
1 tsp crushed ginger
½ tsp chilli powder
1 tsp cumin powder
½ tsp turmeric powder
½ tsp pepper powder
2 green chillies, slit lengthways
2 tsp tamarind paste
2 tbsp cider vinegar
salt to taste
1 cup water

Fry the onions in oil until lightly browned. Add the pork and fry for a further 2 minutes. Then add the rest of the ingredients, cover with water, and simmer on a low heat, stirring occasionally until pork is tender.

Preparation time: 10 minutes
Cooking time: 30 minutes

Roast Pork

Ingredients

4 cloves crushed garlic
1 tsp crushed ginger
1 tsp cumin powder
½ tsp clove powder
½ tsp turmeric powder
2 tbsp lemon juice
½ tsp cinnamon powder
2 tbsp olive oil
1 tbsp cider vinegar
salt & pepper to taste
1 kg pork

Mix all the ingredients together, apply to the pork, and marinate for an hour (the longer the better). Place in the oven at 180°C/350°F/gas mark 4 and roast until cooked.

Preparation time: 10 minutes
Cooking time: 1hr 30 minutes

Roast Beef

Ingredients

4 cloves crushed garlic
1 tsp crushed ginger
½ tsp turmeric powder
½ tsp clove powder
½ tsp cinnamon powder
½ tsp pepper powder
1 tbsp lemon juice
2 tbsp olive oil
salt to taste
1 kg beef

Mix all the ingredients together and apply to the beef. Marinate for an hour or longer. Place in the oven at 180°C/350°F/gas mark 4 and roast until beef is tender.

Preparation time: 10 minutes
Cooking time: 1 hour

Minced Beef Curry

Ingredients

½ kg minced beef
1 onion, finely chopped
2 green chillies, finely chopped
4 cloves crushed garlic
1 tsp crushed ginger
1 tsp cumin powder
1 tbsp coriander powder
1 tbsp tomato puree
½ tsp chilli powder
2 tbsp coriander leaves, chopped
1 tsp tamarind paste
2 cups water
salt & pepper to taste

Cook the mince in a pan on a low heat, stirring continuously for a couple of minutes. Drain off any fat. Add the rest of the ingredients and cook, stirring occasionally.

Preparation time: 10 minutes
Cooking time: 25 minutes

Meat Ball Curry

Ingredients

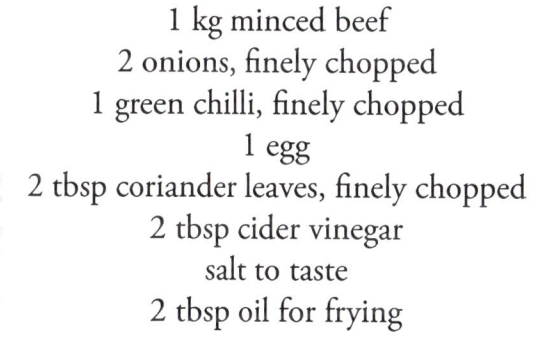

1 kg minced beef
2 onions, finely chopped
1 green chilli, finely chopped
1 egg
2 tbsp coriander leaves, finely chopped
2 tbsp cider vinegar
salt to taste
2 tbsp oil for frying

For the Curry Sauce
1 onion, finely chopped
2 tbsps olive oil
½ tsp chilli powder
½ tsp cinnamon powder
½ tsp clove powder
4 cloves crushed garlic
1 tsp crushed ginger
1 tsp cumin powder
½ tsp turmeric powder
2 tbsp tomato puree
salt & pepper to taste
1 cup water

Mix the minced beef with the onions, green chilli, egg, coriander leaves, vinegar, and salt. Make into little balls, fry, and keep aside. To make the sauce, fry the onion until lightly browned, then add the rest of the ingredients except the water and stir for a few seconds. Add the water and bring to the boil. Finally add the meat balls and gently simmer for 10 minutes, stirring occasionally.

Preparation time: 20 minutes
Cooking time: 20 minutes

Beef Chilli Fry

Ingredients

1 onion, sliced
2 tbsp olive oil
¼ tsp clove powder
½ tsp cumin powder
1 tsp crushed ginger
4 cloves crushed garlic
½ kg beef (boiled & cubed)
1 green chilli, sliced
1 green pepper, sliced
1 tbsp tomato puree
2 tbsp coriander leaves, chopped
2 cups water
salt & pepper to taste

Fry the onion in oil until lightly brown. Add the spices and beef and stir for a few seconds. Add the rest of the ingredients, and cook until the water has been absorbed, stirring frequently.

Preparation time: 20 minutes
Cooking time: 20 minutes

Lamb's Liver

Ingredients

2 tbsp flour
½ tsp cumin powder
1 tsp coriander powder
½ tsp turmeric powder
pinch of chilli powder
salt & pepper to taste
4 slices of lamb's liver
2 tablespoons olive oil

Combine the flour and spices together, then coat the liver slices with the mixture. Heat the oil and fry on both sides until golden brown.

Preparation time: 10 minutes
Cooking time: 10 minutes

Lamb Curry

Ingredients:

1 onion, finely chopped
½ kg lamb, diced
2 tbsps olive oil
4 cloves crushed garlic
1 tsp crushed ginger
1 tbsp coriander powder
1 tsp cumin powder
½ tsp clove powder
½ tsp turmeric powder
½ tsp chilli powder
½ tsp nutmeg powder
½ tsp cinnamon powder
1 green chilli, sliced lengthways
1 tbsp tamarind paste
50 g coconut cream
2 cups water
salt to taste

Fry the onion and the lamb pieces until lightly browned, then add all the spices and stir for a few seconds. Add the coconut cream, cover with water, and simmer, stirring occasionally until the lamb is cooked.

Preparation time: 15 minutes
Cooking time: 30 minutes

Lamb Biryani

Ingredients

1 onion, finely chopped
½ kg lamb, diced
2 tbsp olive oil
1 tsp cumin seeds
2 cloves crushed garlic
1 tsp crushed ginger
½ tsp cumin powder
1 tbsp coriander powder
½ tsp chilli powder
½ tsp turmeric powder
½ tsp cinnamon powder
½ tsp clove powder
1 tbsp tomato puree
2 tbsp coriander leaves, chopped
4 cups water
1 stock cube (vegetable or lamb)
2 cups rice, washed
a few saffron strands
salt & pepper to taste

Fry the onion and the lamb pieces in oil until lightly browned, then add the cumin seeds and the rest of the spices (apart from the rice and saffron strands). Add the water and stock cube, bring to the boil, and simmer for 20 minutes until the lamb is tender. Finally stir in the rice and saffron strands and cover and simmer for a further 10 minutes. Turn off heat but do not remove the cover for another 10 minutes, to let the rice steam. Gently turn with a fork before serving.

Preparation time: 15 minutes
Cooking time: 30 minutes

Roast Lamb

Ingredients

4 cloves crushed garlic
1 tsp crushed ginger
½ tsp turmeric powder
¼ tsp clove powder
¼ tsp cinnamon powder
¼ tsp pepper powder
1 tbsp lemon juice
2 tbsp olive oil
1 tbsp mint sauce
salt to taste
1 kg lamb

Mix all the ingredients together and apply to the lamb. Marinate for an hour or longer. Place in the oven at 180°C/350°F/gas mark 4 and roast until lamb is tender.

Preparation time: 10 minutes
Cooking time: 1 hour 30 minutes

Vegetarian

Cabbage with Coconut

Karela

Chilli-son-Carne

Cashew Nut Stir Fry

Spiced Chickpeas or Black Eye Beans

Dal Curry

Ladyfingers (Okra)

Pumpkin

Aubergines

Carrots, Peas and Potatoes

Mushroom Bhaji

Stuffed Paprika

Cauliflower Cheese

Spinach with Almonds

Breadfruit

Black Eye Bean Salad

Tuna Salad

Salad Dressing

Vegtables And Fruits

A few varieties seen in Mapusa market

Cabbage with Coconut

Ingredients

1 medium sized cabbage, shredded
½ tsp cumin seeds
¼ tsp turmeric powder
¼ tsp paprika powder
1 tbsp desiccated coconut
½ cup water
salt & pepper to taste

Place the shredded cabbage in a pan with all the ingredients. Bring to the boil, stir, and cover with lid. Simmer for 5 minutes. Turn off the heat but leave the cover on for a further 5 minutes before serving.

Preparation time: 5 minutes
Cooking time: 10 minutes

Karela

(Excellent for diabetics and now available in frozen packets)

Ingredients

2 tbsp olive oil
1 onion, finely chopped
½ tsp cumin seeds
1 tsp coriander powder
¼ tsp turmeric powder
salt & pepper to taste
1 tbsp tomato puree
1 green chilli, sliced
3 karelas, sliced and seeded
1 cup water

Heat the oil and fry the onion until lightly browned. Stir in the spices, then add the rest of the ingredients and cook on a low heat, stirring occasionally.

Preparation time: 10 minutes
Cooking time: 15 minutes

Chilli con Carne – Goan Style

Ingredients

1 onion, finely chopped
2 tbsp olive oil
1 tsp cumin seeds
½ tsp cumin powder
4 cloves crushed garlic
1 tsp crushed ginger
1 tbsp coriander powder
½ tsp chilli powder
salt & pepper to taste
500 g soya mince or vegemince
1 tin (400g) tomatoes, chopped
1 tbsp tomato puree
2 ½ cups water
1 tin (400g) kidney beans, drained

Fry the onion in oil until lightly browned, then add the cumin seeds and rest of the spices. Stir for a minute. Add the rest of the ingredients except the beans and cook on a low heat for 10 minutes. Lastly add the kidney beans and simmer for a further 10 minutes.

Preparation time: 10 minutes
Cooking time: 25 minutes

Cashew Nut Stir-Fry

Ingredients

2 tbsp olive oil
1 onion, sliced
½ tsp cumin seeds
½ tsp turmeric powder
½ tsp coriander powder
1 tbsp coriander leaves, chopped
salt & pepper to taste
1 cup cashew nuts
250 g bean shoots
2 carrots, finely sliced
a few mangetout peas
1 red pepper, sliced lengthways
½ cup water

Heat the oil and fry the onion until lightly browned. Add the spices and stir for a few seconds. Stir in the rest of the ingredients and cook for 10 minutes.

Preparation time: 10 minutes
Cooking time: 12 minutes

Spiced Chickpeas or Black-eyed Beans

Ingredients

1 onion, finely chopped
1 tbsp olive oil
¼ tsp chilli powder
¼ tsp turmeric powder
1 tsp cumin powder
1 tbsp coriander powder
4 cloves crushed garlic
1 tsp crushed ginger
2 tbsp coriander leaves, chopped
salt & pepper to taste
1 tin (400g) tomatoes, chopped
50 g coconut cream
1 fresh green chilli (slit lengthways)
1 tbsp tomato puree
250 g beans (black-eye or chick peas, soaked overnight)
1 cup water

The fastest method is to use a pressure cooker to prepare this dish. Fry the onion in oil until lightly browned. Add all the spices and stir for a few seconds. Then add the tinned tomatoes and coconut cream. When the coconut has dissolved, add the rest of the ingredients, including the beans. Cover with water and boil until the beans are soft.

Preparation time: 15 minutes
Cooking time: 30 minutes (in a pressure cooker)

Dal Curry

Ingredients

1 onion, finely chopped
1 tbsp olive oil
½ tsp cumin seeds
1 cup mung dal
¼ tsp turmeric powder
1 tbsp coriander powder
2 cloves crushed garlic
1 tsp crushed ginger
1 green chilli, slit lengthways
1 tbsp tomato puree
2 tbsp coriander leaves, chopped
1 tbsp lemon juice
2 ½ cups water
salt to taste

Fry the onion in oil until lightly browned. Add the cumin seeds and fry for a few seconds, then add the mung dal and the rest of the ingredients. Cover with water and cook until the mung dal is soft, stirring frequently so it doesn't stick to the bottom of the pan.

Preparation time: 10 minutes
Cooking time: 30 minutes

Ladyfingers (Okra)

Ingredients

1 onion, chopped
1 tbsp olive oil
1 tbsp coriander powder
½ tsp turmeric powder
½ tsp cumin seeds
1 green chilli, sliced lengthways
salt to taste
12 ladyfingers, sliced
½ cup water

Fry the onion in oil until lightly browned. Add the spices and stir for a few seconds. Mix in the ladyfingers Add water and cook on a low heat, stirring occasionally.

Preparation time: 10 minutes
Cooking time: 10 minutes

Pumpkin

Ingredients

1 onion, sliced
1 tbsp olive oil
½ tsp cumin seeds
1 small pumpkin, cubed
½ tsp chilli powder
2 tbsp desiccated coconut
1 cup water
salt & pepper to taste

Fry the onion in oil until lightly browned. Add the cumin seeds and stir for a few seconds, then add the pumpkin and the rest of the ingredients. Cook on a low heat, stirring occasionally.

Preparation time: 15 minutes
Cooking time: 15 minutes

Aubergines (Egg Plant)

Ingredients

1 large aubergine
1 egg (beaten)
2 tbsp semolina, for coating
oil for frying
salt & pepper to taste

Slice the aubergine and dip the slices one at a time in the beaten egg and coat with semolina. Shallow fry on both sides until golden brown.

Preparation time: 5 minutes
Cooking time: 10 minutes

Carrots, Peas and Potatoes

Ingredients

1 onion, chopped
1 tbsp olive oil
1 cup frozen peas
1 cup water
1 tsp cumin seeds
½ tsp cumin powder
½ tsp turmeric powder
1 tsp coriander powder
pinch of chilli powder
1 tbsp coriander leaves, finely chopped
1 tbsp tomato puree
2 carrots, sliced
2 potatoes, cubed
salt to taste

Fry the onion in oil until lightly browned. Add the frozen peas and water and all the spices, including the tomato puree, and cook for 5 minutes. Then add the carrots and potatoes and cook for a further 10 minutes, stirring occasionally.

Preparation time: 10 minutes
Cooking time: 17 minutes

Mushroom Bhaji

Ingredients

1 onion, finely chopped
1 tbsp olive oil
1 teaspoon cumin seeds
1 tbsp coriander powder
pinch of chilli powder
2 cloves crushed garlic
1 tbsp coriander leaves, chopped
salt & pepper to taste
250 g whole mushrooms

Fry the onion in oil until lightly browned. Add the spices and stir for a few seconds. Finally, add the mushrooms and cook on a medium heat, stirring occasionally.

Preparation time: 5 minutes
Cooking time: 10 minutes

Stuffed Paprika

Ingredients

2 tbsp olive oil
1 onion, finely chopped
½ kg mince (soya or vege)
2 green chillies, finely chopped
4 cloves crushed garlic
1 tsp crushed ginger
1 tsp cumin powder
1 tbsp coriander powder
1 tbsp tomato puree
½ tsp chilli powder
2 tbsp coriander leaves, chopped
1 tsp tamarind paste
2 cups water
salt & pepper to taste
4 paprikas

Heat the oil and fry the onion until lightly browned. Add the rest of the ingredients except the paprikas and simmer for 15 minutes until the liquid has nearly been absorbed. Wash the paprikas, cut off the tops, and fill with mince. Bake in the oven at 180°C/350°F/gas mark 4 for 45 minutes.

Preparation time: 15 minutes
Cooking time: 1 hour.

Cauliflower Cheese

Ingredients

1 medium cauliflower
½ cup water
salt to taste

For Cheese Sauce

40 g butter or margarine
40 g plain flour
½ tsp cumin powder
½ pt milk
50 g cheese, grated
pinch of paprika powder

Boil the cauliflower for 5 minutes (do not overcook), drain off any water, and place in a dish.

To prepare the cheese sauce, gently melt the butter or margarine, add flour and cumin powder, and stir continuously for a few seconds until the mixture thickens slightly. Then add milk, a little at a time, again stirring continuously. Finally add the grated cheese, still stirring. Pour over lightly cooked cauliflower and sprinkle with paprika.

Preparation time: 10 minutes
Cooking time: 10 minutes

Spinach with Almonds

Ingredients

1 onion, chopped
1 tbsp olive oil
½ tsp cumin powder
pinch of turmeric powder
2 bunches spinach, chopped
½ cup almonds
½ cup water
salt & pepper to taste

Fry the onion in oil until lightly browned. Stir in the cumin and turmeric, then add the spinach, almonds, water, salt, and pepper. Cover and simmer until cooked.

Preparation time: 10 minutes
Cooking time: 10 minutes

Breadfruit

Ingredients

1 breadfruit, peeled and sliced
1 egg, beaten
2 tablespoons semolina
salt & pepper to taste
oil for frying

Dip the pieces of breadfruit in the beaten egg, coat with the semolina, and fry on both sides until golden brown.

Preparation time: 10 minutes
Cooking time: 10 minutes

Black-eyed Bean Salad

Ingredients

2 cups black-eyed beans (soaked overnight)
2 tbsp fresh coriander leaves, finely chopped
½ tsp paprika powder
4 spring onion stalks

For the dressing

2 cloves garlic, crushed
1 tsp mustard
2 tbsp olive oil
2 tbsp cider vinegar
1 tbsp lemon juice
salt & pepper to taste

Cover the beans with water and cook for 30 minutes (in a pressure cooker) until beans are soft. Drain and set aside to cool. Prepare the dressing – mix all the ingredients together and pour over the cooled beans. Stir in the coriander leaves, paprika powder, and spring onions.

Preparation time: 10 minutes
Cooking time: 30 minutes

Tuna Salad

Ingredients

1 tin(185g) tuna, drained
1 tbsp mayonnaise
pinch of black pepper
1 green chilli, seeded and finely chopped
2 spring onion stalks, chopped
1 tbsp coriander leaves, finely chopped
Any salad vegetables desired for garnish

Mix all the ingredients together and spread this mixture into a dish. Decorate with any other salad ingredients you choose.

Salad Dressing

Ingredients

2 tbsp olive oil
2 tbsp cider vinegar
2 cloves garlic, crushed
½ tsp mustard
1 tsp honey
1 tbsp fresh coriander leaves, finely chopped
salt & pepper to taste

Mix all ingredients well. Shake before using.
Chopped coriander leaves in salads give a delicious flavour!

Vegetarian

Rice

Traditional Goa Rice and Curry

Pulao Rice

Vegetable Pulao

Purees

Chappatis

Pickles

Traditional Goa Rice & Curry

Rice and curry was always cooked in earthenware pots over a wood fire, which gave these two dishes their unique flavour.

Ingredients

3 cups water
1 cup Goan rice
salt to taste

Boil the water, then add the washed rice and salt and cook for 30 minutes until rice is soft. Drain away any excess water from the rice before serving.

For the curry

1 coconut, grated
½ tsp turmeric powder
1 tsp coriander powder
¼ tsp cumin powder
3 cloves garlic
5 red kashmiri chillies
2 tsp tamarind paste

Blend all the ingredients together and cook on a slow fire with a little water. For additional flavour, fish, dried mangoes (*solas*), and bimblis can be added.

Pulao Rice

Ingredients

1 tbsp olive oil
1 onion, finely chopped
½ tsp cumin seeds
6 whole peppercorns
1 cinnamon stick
6 whole cloves
4 cardamom pods
3 ½ cups water
¼ tsp turmeric powder
1 stock cube (chicken or vegetable)
2 cups rice (basmati)
2 tbsp coriander leaves, chopped
pinch of saffron strands
salt to taste

Heat the oil and fry the onion until lightly browned. Add the cumin seeds, peppercorns, cinnamon stick, cloves, cardamom pods and stir for a few seconds. Then add water, turmeric powder, and stock cube. When the stock cube has dissolved, add rice, coriander leaves, pinch of saffron strands and salt. Bring to the boil, then cover the pan and turn down heat to the lowest temperature. After 10 minutes turn off the heat and let rice cook with the steam from inside the pan. Do not take off the lid for another 15 minutes. When ready to serve, gently turn the rice with a fork. Remove the cloves, peppercorns, cardamom pods, and cinnamon stick before serving.

Preparation time: 10 minutes
Cooking time: 10 minutes

Vegetable Pulao

Ingredients

1 onion, finely chopped
1 tbsp olive oil
6 cloves
6 peppercorns
½ tsp cumin seeds
1 cardamom stick
1½ cups water
½ tsp turmeric powder
1 stock cube (chicken or vegetable)
½ cup peas or sliced green beans
2 carrots, sliced
2 cups rice
a few saffron strands
1 tbsp coriander leaves, chopped

Fry the onion in oil until lightly browned. Add cloves, peppercorns, cumin seeds, and cardamom stick and stir for a few seconds. Then add the water, turmeric, and stock cube. When the stock cube has dissolved, add the peas and cook for 5 minutes. Lastly add the carrots, rice, saffron strands, and coriander leaves. When the rice has come to the boil, cover the pan and turn down the heat to the lowest temperature. After 10 minutes, turn off the heat and let rice cook with the steam from inside the pan. Do not take off the lid for another 15 minutes. Gently turn the rice with a fork before serving.

Preparation time: 10 minutes
Cooking time: 17 minutes.

Purees

Ingredients

2 cups wheat flour
2 tbsp olive oil
½ tsp salt
water for mixing
oil for frying

Mix the flour, oil, salt, and water to form a soft dough. Sprinkle the work surface with some flour and roll out the dough, making sure it is not too thick. Cut into round shapes with the aid of a cutter. Deep fry in hot oil until lightly brown on both sides.

Preparation time: 10 minutes
Cooking time: 10 Minutes

Chappatis

Ingredients for Chappatis

3 cups wheat chapatti flour
2 tbsp olive oil
water for mixing
½ tsp salt
ghee for frying

Knead the flour, oil, salt and water to form a soft dough. Make into small round balls and roll each ball into a round, thin pancake. These pancakes can be cooked in a non-stick frying pan. Heat the pan and place the chappati down for a few seconds, turn over and brush it with a thin layer of ghee, turn to the other side and repeat. Cook until both sides are golden brown.

Preparation time: 10 minutes
Cooking time: 20 minutes

Pickles

Pickles have always been a great accompaniment to any Goan dish. They are usually made from fruits or vegetables using preserving agents consisting of spices, sugar, oil, and vinegar. My two very favourites are raw mango pickles that my dad used to prepare and carrot pickles made by my mum. Enjoy!

Raw Mango Water Pickle

Ingredients

5 small tender green mangoes
2 tbsp rock salt
2 green chillies, chopped
2 cups water

Wash, slice, and seed the mangos. Add the salt, chillies, water and put in a jar. Keep sealed for a day before eating.

Carrot Pickle

Ingredients

4 lbs carrots
2 tbsp salt
half cup oil
2 oz mustard seeds
1 oz fenugreek seeds
2 oz garlic, crushed
2 oz ginger, crushed
2 oz chilli powder
4 oz green chillies, finely cut
a few curry leaves
1 bottle (350ml) vinegar
sugar & salt to taste

Wash the carrots, cut into strips, mix with salt, and keep overnight. The next day, drain off any liquid and dry in the sun. Next, heat the oil and keep aside. Mix all the ingredients except the carrots and oil and bring to the boil. (The vinegar is the liquid allowing the boil.) Turn off heat, and when cool, stir in the carrots and oil. Pour into a jar, making sure the oil floats above the carrots.

Desserts

Banana Fritters

Avocado Pudding

Semolina Halwa

Gulab Jams (Semolina Balls)

Vonn (Coconut & Jaggery Pudding)

Patholyos

Mango Lassi

Fruit Salad and Cinnamon Custard

Banana Fritters

Ingredients

4 tbsp flour
½ tsp cinnamon powder
1 egg
2 tbsp brown sugar
pinch of salt
½ cup milk
2 large bananas, mashed
2 tbsp sultanas (optional)
2 tbsp olive oil, for frying

Mix the flour with the cinnamon, and add the egg, sugar, salt, and milk to form a thick batter. Then mix in the mashed bananas (and sultanas). Heat the oil and ladle in a spoonful of batter. Fry on both sides until golden brown.

Preparation time: 10 minutes
Cooking time: 3 minutes per fritter

Avocado Pudding

Ingredients

2 fresh avocados
2 tbsp brown sugar
a splash of soya milk (or fresh milk)

Cut the avocado in half, remove seed and peel off the skin. Mash the avocados, add sugar and milk. Serve chilled.

Preparation time: 10 minutes

Semolina Halwa

Ingredients

1 tbsp ghee
4 tbsp (or ½ cup) semolina
½ tsp cinnamon powder
1 pint milk
4 tbsp brown sugar
few drops of colouring, if desired

Melt the ghee in a pan on a medium heat and stir in the semolina and cinnamon powder. Then add milk and stir continuously until the mixture starts to thicken. Finally stir in the sugar. For a festive look, a few drops of colouring can be added. Pour into a bowl and leave to set for an hour.

Preparation time: 5 minutes
Cooking Time: 10 minutes

Gulab Jams (Semolina Balls)

Ingredients

7 tbsp low-fat powdered milk
3 tsp self-raising flour
1 tsp semolina
½ tsp cardamom powder
6 tbsp milk
1½ tbsp ghee
oil for deep frying

For the Syrup

4 tbsp sugar
1 pint water
2 tbsp rose water

Begin by making the syrup. Heat sugar and water until it thickens into a syrup. Stir in the rose water and set aside.

In another bowl, mix the rest of the ingredients, form into small balls, and deep fry until golden brown. Place the balls in the syrup mixture and leave for 2 hours before serving. (Makes around 30 balls.)

Preparation time: 15 minutes
Cooking time: 10 minutes
(Plus 2 hours standing time)

Vonn (Coconut & Jaggery Pudding)

This semi-liquid dessert is truly delicious, nutritious, and very easy to prepare.

Ingredients

½ cup channa dal (soaked overnight)
100 g rice flour
1 tin (400 ml) coconut milk
200 g jaggery (grated)
pinch of salt

Cover the dal with water and boil for 30 minutes until soft. Drain and set aside. Mix the rice flour with coconut milk and bring to the boil. Add jaggery and dal and simmer, stirring continuously, until the mixture thickens. Serve warm.

Preparation time: 10 minutes
Cooking time: 40 minutes.

Patolyos

Patolyos are a very popular steamed rice sweet. For this special dish, the aromatic leaves of the turmeric plant are used, which gives it a truly unique flavour. The leaves are washed, trimmed, and coated with a thin layer of rice batter, followed by another layer of coconut and jaggery. The leaf is then folded and steamed. Once tasted, never forgotten!

Ingredients

5 turmeric leaves (washed and trimmed)

For the Rice Batter

1 cup rice flour
½ tsp salt
½ cup water

For the Filling

1 cup fresh coconut, grated
½ cup jaggery gratings
½ tsp cardamom powder
a few raisins

Mix the rice, salt, and a little water to make a thick batter. Line up the leaves on a clean work surface and spread the batter thinly over them. Next, mix the coconut, jaggery, cardamom and raisins and put it in a thin layer in the middle of the leaves. Fold the leaves over and press lightly around the leaf so the batter sticks together. Place in a steamer for 15 minutes.

Preparation time: 1 hour
Cooking time: 15 minutes

Mango Lassi

Ingredients

250 ml milk
250 ml plain yoghurt
1 tbsp honey
4 mango slices, mashed

Whisk the milk, yoghurt and honey for 2 minutes, then stir in the mashed mango. Serve chilled. Lassi is a very cooling drink and can be prepared plain or with other soft fruits.

Fruit Salad

Ingredients

1 ripe papaya, diced
2 bananas, sliced
1 apple, sliced
1 ripe mango, cubed
Seeds of 2 Passion Fruits

Mix all the fruits together and serve with cold cinnamon custard.

For Cinnamon Custard

500 ml milk
2 tbsp custard powder,
1 tbsp brown sugar
½ tsp cinnamon powder.

Mix all the ingredients together and bring to the boil, stirring continuously. When it begins to thicken, turn off heat and leave to cool.

Goan Sweets

Spiced Fruit Cake

Bibinca

Dodol

Coconut & Semolina Cake

Almond Cookies

Doce (Dal Sweet)

Kulkuls

Coconut Cookies

Neureos

Seed Cup Cakes

Ribbon Cake

DECEMBER – the month for feasting! In many countries, December is the highlight of the food calendar. In Goa everyone does their best to make the current year outshine the previous year with bigger, better, tastier spreads – and the month provides a lot of good excuses to do this!

It starts December 3 in celebrating the feast of Saint Francis Xavier, the patron saint of Goa and an inspiration to Catholics everywhere due to his lifetime of tireless work and missions to foreign countries. The day is celebrated with all the colour, flavour, and noise that the state can muster. Old Goa, where the basilica which houses Saint Francis's body is, is filled with dedicated visitors who come to pay their respects to him and to celebrate his many miraculous achievements. Naturally, the celebrations culminate in many feasts – people savouring the flavours of Goa's traditional dishes, such as sorpotel and xacuti, with sannas to mop up the curry sauce.

Outside and around the basilica, stalls are set up selling the famous sweetmeats such as ladoos, grams, and jaggery-based sweets.

December is also the favoured month for weddings. Many Goans have emigrated to countries such as Canada, Australia, and the United Kingdom, so this month becomes the perfect point to get all the family back together. And how best to celebrate? More feasting! The wedding reception venues are always dominated by long tables covered in all the favourites, like fish curry and steaming bowls of pulao rice. Then there are big celebratory dinners at the homes of the happy couple's parents during the following week. (A chance, I think, to show which mother-in-law is the better cook!)

Finally of course, there is Christmas itself. Being a predominantly Catholic state, Christmas is widely celebrated in every town and village. On Christmas Day, many of the traditional sweets such as bibinca, dodol, neuros and doce are shared with family, friends and neighbours to celebrate the festive season.

Spiced Fruit Cake

Ingredients
1 sachet green tea
1 cup hot water
500 g dried mixed fruits
2 tsp ground mixed spice
250 g butter
200 g dark brown sugar
6 eggs
few drops of vanilla essence
2 tbsp brandy or ginger wine
100 g glace cherries, sliced
400 g self-raising flour
25 g almonds

Prepare the green tea in the hot water. Place the mixed fruits in a bowl, add one teaspoon mixed spice and the green tea. Stir thoroughly and leave to soak overnight.

When ready to bake, mix the butter and sugar until light and fluffy, then add the eggs one at a time. Add the other teaspoon of mixed spice, vanilla essence, and brandy or ginger wine. Mix thoroughly. Slice the cherries and, in a separate bowl, coat with a tablespoon of flour. Finally, add half the quantity of flour into the mixture followed by half of the mixed fruits, cherries, and almonds. Mix thoroughly. Add the rest of the flour and fruits and mix thoroughly. Pour the mixture into a baking tray and place in a preheated oven at 160°C/325°F/gas mark 3 until baked. (To test whether it is baked through, put a knife through the centre. If the knife comes out wet with mixture, the cake needs further baking).

Preparation time: 20 minutes (plus overnight soaking)
Cooking time: 1 hr 45 minutes

Bibinca

Ingredients

800 ml coconut milk
1 cup brown sugar
6 egg yolks
½ tsp cardamom powder
pinch of nutmeg powder
1 cup plain flour
½ cup ghee

Mix the coconut milk with sugar, then add the egg yolks and spices. Stir in the flour to make a thick batter and let it stand for 10 minutes. Heat a tablespoon of ghee in a baking pan under the grill. Pour a thin layer of batter into the pan and grill for a few minutes till the batter is cooked and light brown in colour. Remove the pan from the grill and put another spoonful of ghee over the cooked layer and pour in another layer of batter and place under the grill. Repeat this process till all the batter has been used. Aim for 6–7 layers. Cool before cutting into slices.

Preparation time: 15 minutes
Cooking time: 1 hour

Dodol

Ingredients

2 tbsp ghee
100 g rice flour
800 ml coconut milk
200 g coconut jaggery, grated
100 g cashew nuts, chopped

Melt the ghee, then stir in the rice flour and coconut milk. When the mixture thickens, add the jaggery and nuts and continue stirring until mixture begins to leave the sides of the pan. Pour into a dish and leave to cool.

Preparation time: 10 minutes
Cooking time: 20 minutes

Coconut & Semolina Cake

Ingredients

250 g butter
200 g brown sugar
4 eggs
1 tsp cardamom powder
1 ½ tsp caraway seeds
2 tbsp rose water
¼ pt milk
100 g desiccated coconut
250 g semolina
1 tsp baking powder

Mix the butter and sugar until light and fluffy, then add the eggs one at a time. Add the cardamom, caraway, rose water, and milk. Lastly add the coconut, semolina, and baking powder. Mix thoroughly and bake in a preheated oven at 160°C/325°F/gas mark 3.

Preparation time: 20 minutes
Cooking time: 1 hour

Almond Cookies

Ingredients

1 cup self-raising flour
½ cup ground almonds
2 tbsp soft brown sugar
½ tsp cardamom powder
2 tbsp ghee or butter
few drops of almond essence

Mix all the ingredients together to form a soft dough. Roll into little balls with the palm of your hand and place onto a baking tray. Place in the oven at 160°C/325°F/gas mark 3, and bake for 20 minutes.

Preparation time: 15 minutes
Cooking time: 20 Minutes

Doce (Dal Sweet)

Ingredients

½ kg channa dal (soaked overnight)
3 tbsp desiccated coconut
3 tbsp brown sugar
2 tbsp ghee

Cover the channa dal with water and boil until soft. Drain and mash the dal. Heat ghee in a pan and add the sugar and coconut. Stir in the dal and cook until the mixture thickens and starts to leave the sides of the pan. Pour onto a plate to cool.

Cooking time: 45 minutes

Kulkuls

Ingredients

1 cup semolina
½ cup plain flour
1 egg
1 tbsp butter
2 tbsp brown sugar
½ tsp cardamom powder
2 tbsp water for mixing
Oil for frying

Mix all the ingredients together to form a ball of soft dough. Take a small bit and press into a fork and roll into a shape of a cowrie shell. Deep fry until light brown.

Preparation time: 30 minutes
Cooking time: 10 minutes

Coconut Cookies

Ingredients

½ cup semolina
½ cup desiccated coconut
3 eggs
3 tbsp brown sugar
1 tbsp rose water
2 tbsp butter

Mix all the ingredients together to form a soft dough. Form into little balls in the palm of your hands and bake in the oven at 160°C/325°F/gas mark 3

Preparation time: 15 minutes
Cooking time: 30 minutes

Neuroeos

Ingredients

½ kg plain flour
2 tbsp ghee
pinch of salt
½ cup water

For the Filling

2 tbsp ghee
½ kg semolina
3 tbsp desiccated coconut
3 tbsp brown sugar
½ tsp cardamom powder
3 tbsp ground sesame seeds
oil for frying

First make the pastry by mixing the flour, ghee, salt and water to form a soft dough.

For the filling, heat the ghee and fry semolina and desiccated coconut, stirring continuously, until the mixture is quite dry. Then add the sugar, sesame seeds and cardamom. Leave aside to cool.

Roll out the pastry and cut into round shapes. Put a spoonful of the filling into each, wet the edges of the pastry, and press down to form half-moon shapes. Deep fry on both sides until light brown.

Preparation time: 1 hour
Cooking time: 15 minutes

Seed Cup Cakes

Ingredients

250 g butter or margarine
200 g brown sugar
4 eggs
1 tsp caraway seeds
100 g cherries
few drops of vanilla essence
400 g self-raising flour
2 fl oz milk

Marzipan (for decoration)

Mix the butter and sugar till light and creamy. Add the eggs one at a time. Then add the caraway seeds, cherries and vanilla essence. Stir in the flour and milk. Pour mixture in the cups and bake in a preheated oven at 160°C/325°F/gas mark 3.

Roll out the marzipan on a clean work surface and using various design cutters, decorate the cup cakes.

Preparation time: 15 minutes
Cooking time: 25 minutes

Ribbon Cake

Ingredients

250 g butter
200 g sugar
4 eggs
a few drops of vanilla essence
400 g self-raising flour
3 different colours (green, red, yellow)

Mix the butter and sugar until light and fluffy. Add the eggs, one at a time, and mix well. Add the vanilla essence and finally stir in the flour. Divide the mixture into 3 bowls. Add a few drops of colour into each bowl and mix thoroughly. Pour one part into a baking tray, followed by the other two and bake in a preheated oven at 160°C/325°F/gas mark 3.

Preparation time: 15 minutes
Cooking time: 45 minutes

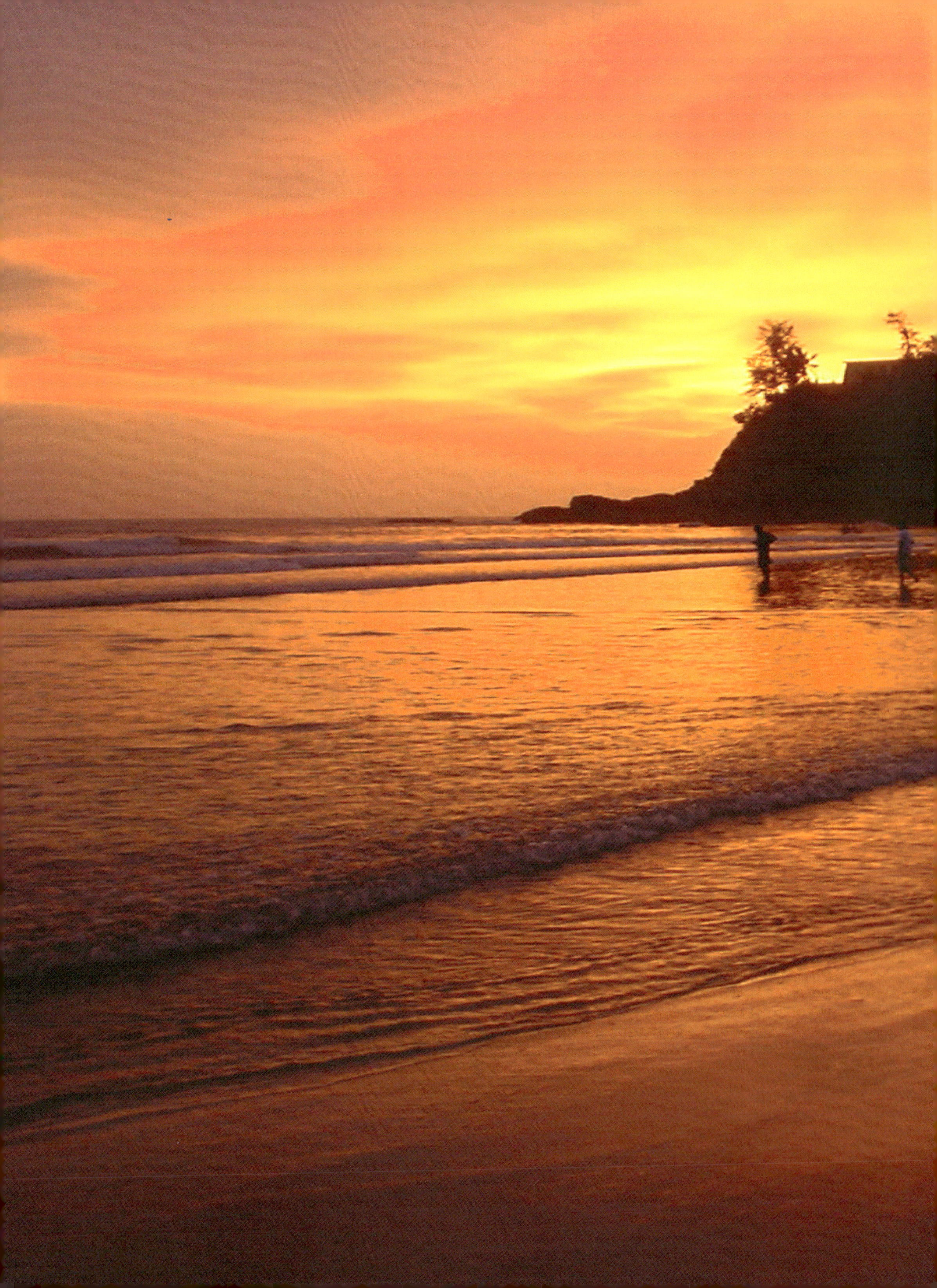

RITA GONSALVES was born in Entebbe, Uganda, and then raised in Goa, India. She has spent her whole life surrounded by wonderful cooks and delicious food and always hoped to one day publish her own recipes. Despite moving to London later in life, she still has very strong ties with her home country and visits her large family in Goa as often as possible.

CPSIA information can be obtained
at www.ICGtesting.com
Printed in the USA
LVIC06n1934301213
367460LV00014B/154